The Spiralizer Recipe Cookbook

by Katey Goodrich

Medical Disclaimer

This book is not intended as a substitute for the medical advice of physicians. The reader should regularly consult a physician in matters relating to his/her health and particularly with respect to any symptoms that may require diagnosis or medical attention.

Table of Contents

Introduction
How Does A Spiralizer Work?
Cleaning and Maintaining a Spiralizer
The 3 Blade Attachments and What They Do
How to Prepare Veggies For Spiralizing
Spiralizer Recipes

Bolognese Zucchini Spaghetti
Sweet Potato Fettuccini al Pesto
Zucchini Fettuccini Carbonara
Zucchini Spaghetti with Seafood
Traditional Wheat Free Lasagna
Sweet Potato Macaroni with Cheese
Zucchini Fettuccini Alfredo
Zucchini Pasta with Six Herb Sauce
Zucchini and Carrot Noodle Soup
Zucchini Pasta Salad
Sweet Potato Pasta with Mushrooms
Zucchini Pasta with Eggplant and Chili
Zucchini Pasta and Mango Chicken Salad
Sweet Potato Pasta with Avocado Sauce
Zucchini Pasta with Fresh Tomato Sauce
Sweet Potato Noodles with Garlic and Olive Oil
Quick Budget Hot Winter Soup
Shanghai Cucumber Noodle Salad
Tuscan Pasta Salad with Basil Pesto
Vegetarian Zucchini Rice

Zesty Butternut Squash Minestrone
Butternut Squash Pasta Fagioli
Sweet Potato, Zucchini and Onion Soup
Creamy Carrot Coleslaw
Healthy Raw Beet and Sweet Potato Salad
Casablanca Sweet Potato Stew
Kagawa Zucchini Udon Noodle Soup
Raw Vegan Zesty Cucumber Ribbon Salad
Asian Fusion Cucumber Noodle Salad
Raw Carrot Noodles with Zesty Lime Peanut Sauce
Oriental Chicken with Carrot Noodles
Zucchini Spaghetti and Meatballs

Conclusion

Introduction

Hi, my name is Katey Goodrich.

I simply love thin curly vegetable noodles. These raw vegetable noodles and salads have worked great for my dieting program. When I started my diet program about six months ago, I invested in a Spiralizer.

This magic slicer tool has then worked wonderfully to serve not only healthy but eye catching salads and vegetable noodles.

Everyone in my family was surprised to see my persistence in this vegetable diet, thanks to the Spiralizer. It has helped reduce the food preparation time and it makes the food so fresh and healthy that you want to take use it every single day.

For that reason, I created this book to share my passion about the Spiralizer slicer and how everyone can use it to prepare, fantastic vegetarian pasta and noodles, healthy salads and vegetable garnishing.

I hope you'll find this book useful and do drop by from time to time for more tips, videos, how-to, and reviews on the Spiralizer.

Katey Goodrich

How Does A Spiralizer Work?

When processing food with a spiralizer there are three very quick and easy stages you need to complete. Firstly take the right size piece of vegetable. Then you place it and make sure it is secure on the spiralizer prongs.

Now after securing the vegetable in position you just turn the spiralizer handle to spiralize the vegetable into the desired shape.

Spiralizers are available in two basic formats; the horizontal or vertical ones. What this refers to is the direction in which the item that you spiralize will travel. Some people find that the vertical type with gravity assisting the shaping process is easier to use but the horizontal type is by far the most popular.

When looking for a spiralizer the good quality ones are those that have several interchangeable blade cartridges allowing you the chance to make vegetarian spaghetti, spirals or other shaped slices when used.

Cleaning and Maintaining a Spiralizer

Use a wet cloth to clean the outer body after each use. Use light and mild detergent to clean the slicer. It is also a good idea to keep it under the running water so that those hard to reach areas get cleaned to some extent.

When cleaning, make sure no food crumbs are left inside the spiral slicer. Use a new medium toothbrush for those stubborn bits of crud you can't reach with a cloth, does the job really well.

Clean the slicer blades too and dry them with dry cloth before storing them. Keep your fingers away from the blade edges, very sharp.

Don't keep them wet for long time, as this will develop rust. If you follow these simple cleaning practices, a spiralizer will last a long time.

The whole unit will go into the dishwasher as well. Be careful handling the blades.

Since a spiralizer it is used for food preparation, it is of prime importance that it is always kept cleaned and maintained well. Some of the important parts of a spiral slicer are the vegetable holder, blades, the rotating handle, catch container and the main body, which holds all these different parts in place.

Hygiene of all these parts is crucial to ensure that the food produced from the spiralizer is contaminant free and safe to consume.

The cranking handle is the most commonly broken part of a spiralizer. Avoid applying too much pressure to the crank handle, it is not necessary, if the vegetable is properly positioned then gentle pressure is all you need to spiralize properly.

An important thing to remember when planning to buy a spiralizer is that you are buying a kitchen appliance, which is mainly made of plastic. And like any other plastic item it has its pros and cons.

Plastic is easy to clean but at same time it can develop cracks easily if given high pressure or dropped from hand. This applies to spiralizer too. Cases of it slipping off the table are common.

Avoid this by making sure the suction pads are always firmly in place before spiralizing.

The 3 Blade Attachments and What They Do

The spiraliser vegetable cutter has 3 interchangeable blades for making vegetable spaghetti noodles, fat veggie noodles, and ribbons from different fruits and veggies.

In each recipe i refer to which blade to use for the recipe, A,B or C.

Blade A:
Blade A is the blade with the small raised prongs.

Blade B:
Blade B is the blade with the large raised prongs.

Blade C:
Blade C is the single blade without prongs, it makes veggie and fruit ribbons and slices.

For future referance you should mark each blade, A, B and C, with an indelible kitchen sharpie. Much easier rather than refering back to this page all the time.

How to Prepare and Cook Veggies for Spiralizing

Zucchini

Slice off ends and cut in half. Can be cooked or eaten raw. Sauté in a skillet for 3 minutes. Simmer in broth for 2 minutes. Can be used for noodles, pasta, salads, slaws.

Sweet Potato

Peel, Slice off ends and cut in half. Can be cooked or eaten raw. Sauté in a skillet for 7 minutes. Simmer in sauce for 6 minutes. Boil for 3 minutes. Bake at 415 for 15 minutes. Can be used for noodles, pasta, chips, curly fires, salads, slaws.

Butternut Squash

Peel, Slice off ends and cut in half. Cooked. Sauté in a skillet for 7 minutes. Simmer in broth for 8 minutes. Bake at 400 for 8 minutes. Can be used for noodles, pasta.

Carrots

Peel, Slice off ends and cut in half. Can be cooked or eaten raw. Boil 3 minutes. Simmer in broth for 8 minutes. Simmer in sauce 6 minutes. Bake at 415 for 11 minutes. Can be used for noodles, pasta, curly fries, chips, salads and slaws.

White Potato

Peel, Slice off ends and cut in half. Cooked. Sauté in a skillet for 7 minutes. Simmer in broth for 8 minutes. Simmer in sauce 6 minutes. Bake at 400 for 15 minutes. Can be used for noodles, pasta, fries and chips.

Cucumber

Slice off ends and cut in half. Eaten raw. Remove excess moisture by pressing with paper towels. Can be used for noodles and salads.

Beets

Peel and slice off ends. Can be cooked or eaten raw. Sauté in a skillet for 6 minutes. Simmer in broth for 7 minutes. Bake at 415 for 12 minutes. Boil for 3 minutes. Can be used for noodles, pasta, chips, salads and slaws.

Rutabaga

Peel and slice off ends and cut in half if larger than normal. Cooked. Sauté in a skillet for 7 minutes. Simmer in broth for 8 minutes. Simmer in sauce 6 minutes. Bake at 400 for 15 minutes. Can be used for noodles, pasta, fries and chips.

Kohlrabi

Peel and slice off ends and cut in half if larger than normal. Cooked and raw. Sauté in a skillet for 7 minutes. Bake at 400 for 15 minutes. Can be used for noodles, pasta, fries and chips.

Parsnips

Peel and Slice off ends and cut in half. Cooked. Sauté in a skillet for 6 minutes. Simmer in broth for 6 minutes. Bake at 415 for 12 minutes. Can be used for noodles, pasta, fries and chips.

Jicama

Peel and Slice off ends and cut in half. Can be cooked or eaten raw. Sauté in a skillet for 6 minutes. Simmer in broth for 6 minutes. Bake at 415 for 12 minutes. Can be used for noodles, pasta, salads, slaws, fries and chips.

Daikon Radish

Peel and Slice off ends and cut in half. Can be cooked or eaten raw. Sauté in a skillet for 6 minutes. Simmer in broth for 6 minutes. Bake at 415 for 12 minutes. Can be used for noodles, pasta, salads, fries and chips.

Eggplant

Slice off ends and cut in half. Cooked. Sauté in a skillet for 6 minutes. Can be used for noodles and pasta. One of the more difficult veggies to spiralize.

Plantain

Peel and Slice off ends and cut in half. Cooked. Simmer in broth for 6 minutes. Bake at 400 for 15 minutes. Can be used for noodles, fries and chips.

Celeriac

Slice off ends at the root, If large cut in half. Cooked. Sauté in a skillet for 6 minutes. Simmer in broth for 6 minutes. Bake at 415 for 12 minutes. Can be used for noodles, pasta, and chips.

Apples

Slice off ends and cut in half. Can be cooked or eaten raw. Bake at 400 for 10 minutes. Sautee in a skillet for 6 minutes. Can be used for snacks, desserts and salads.

Pears

Slice off ends and cut in half. Can be cooked or eaten raw. Sauté in a skillet for 6 minutes, Bake for 10 minutes, Can be used for snacks, desserts, salads and slaws.

Spiralizer Recipes

The Spiralizer Cookbook has over 30 delicious, healthy and easy to prepare spiralizer recipes to start you off with. There are breakfast, lunch and dinner recipes that you and your family will enjoy every week.

I have included recipes that are suitable for people on special diets such as, Vegetarian, Paleo, Wheat free, Low-carb, Vegan, Weight loss, gluten free, low gi, raw food, diabetes and heart healthy.

Each recipe is marked at the bottom for which diet it is friendly for.

Bolognese Zucchini Spaghetti

6 servings

Ingredients:
1 pound (500 grams) of zucchini spaghetti, spiralized (blade a)
Grated parmesan cheese (optional)

Bolognese sauce:
2 table spoons of olive oil
1 mashed clove of garlic
1 onion, minced
1 pound (500 grams) of ground beef
450 grams (1 can) of tomato puree
¼ cup (60 ml) of red wine or water
1 tablespoon of fresh oregano or ½ teaspoon of dry oregano
1 tablespoon of fresh thyme, minced or ½ teaspoon of dry thyme
Freshly ground black pepper

Preparation:
1. Sauce: Heat he oil in a frying pan at medium heat and sauté the garlic and onions for 3 minutes or until the onions soften.
2. Add the meat and cook for 5-7 minutes or until it loses its color. Add the tomato puree, wine or water, oregano & thyme. Lower the heat and leave boiling slightly for 15-20 minutes or until the sauce decreases and thickens. Season with black pepper
3. Cook the pasta 'al dente' in plenty of boiling water with salt. Drain well. Serve the pasta hot covered with the sauce and parmesan cheese (if you use it)

Note: Leave out the beef for vegetarian version, use vegan cheese for vegan

Paleo, Wheat free, Low-carb

Sweet Potato Fettuccini al Pesto

4 servings

Ingredients:
1 pound (500 grams) of sweet potato noodles, spiralized (blade a)

Basil pesto:
1 cup (100 grams) of fresh parmesan cheese, minced
2 mashed cloves of garlic
½ cup (60 grams) of pine nuts
1 large fist of basil (only use the leaves)
¼ cup (60 ml) of olive oil

Preparation:
1. Cook the noodles 'al dente' with plenty of boiling water and salt. Drain and keep hot.
2. Pesto: In a food processor blend the parmesan cheese with the garlic, pine nuts and basil leaves. With the processor on add the olive oil, little by little until you get a smooth paste. Serve the hot pasta with tablespoons of pesto and mix.

Note
Basil is very popular in Italian cooking. Prepare this pesto when there is plenty of basil, then you can freeze it and heat it up in winter.

Paleo, Wheat free, Low-carb

Zucchini Fettuccini Carbonara

4 servings

Ingredients
3 cups (500) grams of zucchini fettuccini, spralized (blade b)

Carbonara Sauce:
1 ½ cups (250 grams) of raw or cooked ham, minced
1 cup (125 ml) of chicken broth
1 cup (250 ml) of thick cream
7 eggs, slightly beaten
2 tablespoons of parsley, minced
Freshly ground black pepper

Preparation:
1. Cook the pasta 'al dente' in plenty of boiling water with salt, drain and keep hot.
2. Sauce: Fry the ham of bacon in a pan, at medium heat for 3 minutes.
3. Add the broth and cream, put the heat on minimum and cook until the sauce decreases.
4. Take the pan off the fire, beat the sauce with the eggs, parsley and pepper. Put back on the fire and cook for 1 minute, mixing constantly, add the hot pasta, mix well and serve right away.

Note:
This is a heavy meal, which is why it should be accompanied with a green-leaf salad.

Paleo, Wheat free, Low-carb

Zucchini Spaghetti with Seafood

4 servings

Ingredients:
3 cups (500 grams) of zucchini spaghetti, spiralized (blade a)
2 teaspoons of olive oil
2 teaspoons of almond butter (or normal)
2 onions, minced
3 ½ cups (850 grams) of tomatoes, peeled, seedless & minced (fresh or canned)
2 tablespoons of fresh basil leaves or 1 teaspoon of dry basil
¼ cup (60 ml) of dry white wine
12 clams, well washed and scrubbed
½ cup (125 grams) of fish fillets, diced
12 raw shrimp, pealed and gutted
½ cup (125 grams) of squid rings

Preparation:
1. Cook the zucchini pasta 'al dente' in plenty of boiling water with salt. Drain & keep hot.
2. Heat oil and butter in a frying pan at medium heat, Sauté the onions until golden.
3. Add the tomato, basil and wine. Lower the heat and let it boil for 8 minutes. Add the clean clams, the fish and shrimp; and cook for 5 more minutes.
4. Add squid, and cook for 1 minute or until the seafood is cooked. Cover the pasta with the mix and serve right away.

Note
This is another traditionally favorite dish, where seafood & fish can be used at your preference. The tomato sauce can be made in advance and kept frozen. While the pasta cooks, unfreeze and heat the sauce and add the seafood like the recipe explains.

Paleo, Wheat free,

Traditional Wheat Free Lasagna

6 servings

Ingredients:
6 zucchinis, ribboned (blade c) (doesn't need cooking)
1 cup of mozzarella cheese, grated

Cheese sauce:
1 small cup of butter
1/3cup (45 grams) of almond flour
2 cups (500 ml) of milk
2 cups grams of strong cheese (cheddar type), grated
Freshly ground black pepper

Meat sauce:
2 tablespoons of olive oil
2 onions, minced
2 mashed cloves of garlic
2 pounds (1.25 kilos) of ground beef
2 pounds (1.25 kilos) of peeled tomatoes, seedless and minced (fresh or canned)
¾ cup (185 ml) of red wine
2 tablespoons of mixed herbs, minced

Preparation:
1. Cheese sauce: Heat the butter in a pot at medium heat. Add the flour and mix for 1 minute. Tale off the fire, add the milk, beat, place back on the fire and cook mixing nonstop until it thickens. Add the cheese; season with black pepper. Mix well and set aside.
2. Meat sauce: Heat oil in a frying pan at medium heat. Sauté the onions and garlic for 3-4 minutes or until the onions soften. Add the meat and sauté for 5-7 minutes or until it loses its color. Add the tomatoes, wine and herbs. Boil at low heat, mixing often, until the sauce thickens and decreases slightly in size, Season to your preference.
3. Cover the bottom of a greased lasagna dish with ribbons of zucchini lasagna. Add a fourth of the meat sauce and a fourth of the

cheese sauce. Repeat these layers until you finish with the
ingredients and cheese sauce.
4. Sprinkle the mozzarella on the top and bake for 30-40 minutes or
until the cheese is golden and makes bubbles.

Note:
Oven temperature 200C
Lasagna is great when accompanied with a steamed vegetable salad.

Paleo, Wheat free, Low-carb

Sweet Potato Macaroni with Cheese

4 servings

Ingredients:
1 pound (500 grams) of spiralized, chopped sweet potato noodles (blade b)
2 cups of cheddar type of cheese, grated

Cheese sauce:
2/3 cup (90 grams) of butter
1/3 cup (45 grams) of flour
1 tablespoon of dry mustard
2 ½ cups (600 ml) of milk
2 cups of cheddar type cheese, grated
Freshly ground black pepper

Preparation:
1. Cook the chopped pasta in boiling water with salt. Drain well and place in a greased pan.
2. Sauce: Melt the butter in a pot at medium heat. Add the flour and mustard, mix for 1 minute. Take off the fire, pour in the milk and beat to mix well. Place back on the fire, at low heat, mixing constantly until it thickens. Add the cheese and season with black pepper
3. Pour the sauce over the pasta, sprinkle with rest of cheese and bake for 20-25 minutes or until the cheese is golden and the pasta is hot.

Note:
Oven temperature 180C
You can transform this popular dish adding some ham, bell peppers, onions or finely minced parsley.

Vegetarian, Paleo, Low-carb

Zucchini Fettuccini Alfredo

4 servings

Ingredients
5 cups of zucchini noodles, spiralized (blade b)
½ cup of melted butter
1 cup of fresh parmesan cheese, grated
Freshly ground black pepper

Preparation
1. Cook the zucchini pasta in boiling water with salt. Drain well and keep hot on a large plate.
2. Distribute melted butter and parmesan cheese over the hot pasta. Season with black pepper, mix and serve right away.

Note:
So simple and yet delicious, If you want a complete meal serve with a well seasoned green leaf salad.

Vegetarian, Paleo, Wheat free, Low-carb

Zucchini Pasta with Six Herb Sauce

4 servings

Ingredients
5 cups of spiralized zucchini pasta (blade a)

Six herb sauce:
3 tbsp olive oil
2 tablespoons fresh rosemary, minced
12 leaves of baby spinach
12 leaves of fresh basil
2 tablespoons of fresh marjoram
2 tablespoons of fresh oregano leaves
2 tablespoons of fresh parsley leaves
2 cloves of garlic, minced
¼ cup (50 ml) of white wine
¼ cup (50 ml) of vegetable broth

Preparation:
1. Cook the zucchini pasta 'al dente' in boiling water with salt. Drain and keep hot.
2. Sauce: Heat oil in a frying pan at medium heat. Sauté for 1-2 minutes the rosemary, baby spinach, basil, marjoram, oregano, garlic and parsley.
3. Add the broth and wine. Lower the flame and simmer for 4 minutes. Serve this sauce over the pasta and mix slightly.

Note:
It is equally delicious as a light meal or starter in a formal dinner, this dish must only be made using fresh herbs not dry ones. You can change the herbs depending what you find in each season: if you can only find four of the herbs mentioned in the recipe, use those only.

Vegetarian, Paleo, Wheat free, Low-carb, Vegan, Weight loss

Zucchini and Carrot Noodle Soup

4 servings

Ingredients:
2 tablespoons of olive oil
1 onion, minced
2 red chilies, fresh, seedless and finely minced
1 red bell pepper, minced
2 carrots, peeled, spiralized (blade a)
2 zucchinis, spiralized (blade b)
4 cups (1 lt.) of vegetable broth
450 grams (2 cups) of tomatoes, pealed, seedless and mashed (or 8 fresh)
450 grams (2 cups) of cooked and drained beans (fresh or canned)
1 tablespoon of fresh thyme, minced or ½ teaspoon of dry thyme
200 grams (1 cup) of tofu (soy cheese), minced
Freshly ground black pepper

Preparation:
1. Heat oil in a frying pan, at medium heat. Sauté the onions and chilies for 3-4 minutes or until the onion softens.
2. Add the red bell pepper, carrots, zucchini, broth, tomatoes and pasta. Lower the heat and cook for 15 minutes or until the pasta is ready.
3. Add the rinsed and drained beans, thyme and tofu. Cook at low heat for 3 more minutes or until the soup is hot, season with black pepper.

Note:
This nutritious and tasty vegetable & pasta soup is by it self a complete meal. In soups you can chop and use all the little leftovers from spiralizing.

Vegetarian, Paleo, Wheat free, Low-carb, Vegan, Weight loss

Zucchini Pasta Salad

4 servings

Ingredients:
500 grams (3 big cups) of spiralized zucchini noodles (blade a)
200 grams (1 cup) of tomatoes, finely sliced
200 grams (1 cup) of artichoke hearts, minced
75 grams of dry chili or fried bell peppers, pealed and minced
125 grams (1/2 cup) of black olives
12 leaves of fresh basil
60 grams (1/4 cup) of parmesan cheese peelings
1-2 tablespoons of olive oil
3 table spoons of vinegar

Preparation:
1. Cook the noodles in boiling water with salt. Drain, rinse and let it cool.
2. In a salad bowl place the pasta, tomatoes, pieces of artichoke, olives, bell pepper or dry chili, basil and parmesan cheese, oil and vinegar. Mix slightly. Cover and refrigerate until it is served.

Note
This delicious salad mixes the best flavors of Italy. Tastes better when prepared the day before so the flavors have time to blend

Vegetarian, Paleo, Wheat free, Low-carb, Weight loss

Sweet Potato Pasta with Mushrooms

4 servings

Ingredients
4 cups of sweet potato noodles (blade b)
2 tablespoons of olive oil
1 mashed clove of garlic
4 cups of fresh mushrooms

White sauce
30 grams of butter
2 tablespoons of almond flour (or regular)
2 cups of almond milk (or regular)
½ teaspoon of ground nutmeg
Freshly ground black pepper

Preparation:
1. Spiralize and Cook the pasta 'al dente' in boiling water with salt. Drain and keep hot.
2. Sauce: Melt the butter in a pan at medium heat. Add the flour and mix for 1 minute. Take off the fire, add the milk and beat until smooth. Place back on the fire and stir constantly until it thickens, season with nutmeg and pepper. Pour over the pasta, mix and keep hot.
3. Heat oil in a frying pan at medium heat and sauté the garlic and mushrooms for 5-6 minutes or until the mushrooms soften. Serve the pasta with the mushroom mix. Serve

Vegetarian, Paleo, Wheat free, Low-carb, Weight loss

Zucchini Pasta with Eggplant and Chili

4 servings

Ingredients:
2 tender eggplants
Salt and pepper
4 cups of spiralized zucchini noodles (blade a)
¼ cup (60 ml) of olive oil
2 onions shredded (blade c)
2 red fresh chilies, seedless and minced
2 cans of mashed tomatoes (or fresh), not drained
½ cup (125 ml) dry white wine
2 tablespoons of fresh basil, minced or 1 teaspoon of dry basil

Preparation:
1. Cut the eggplant in cubes of 2 x2 cm. Place in a colander, sprinkle salt and let it drain for 10-15 minutes. Rinse and dry the cubes.
2. Cook the pasta 'al dente' in plenty of water with salt. Drain and keep hot.
3. Heat oil in a frying pan at medium heat and fry the eggplant in batches until they are golden. Take out of the pan and set aside.
4. In the same pan fry the unions, garlic and chilies, for 3-4 minutes or until the onion softens. Add the tomato, wine and basil; lower the heat and cook for 5 minutes.

Note: Serve this sauce over the eggplant and over the pasta.

Vegetarian, Paleo, Wheat free, Low-carb, Vegan, Weight loss

Zucchini Pasta and Mango Chicken Salad

4 large servings

Ingredients:
1 pound (500 grams) of zucchini noodles, spiralized (blade a)
2 cooked chicken breasts; cut in cubes
8 oz (225 grams) of chestnuts, sliced
8 oz (225 grams) of mango pulp (if canned, drained)

Mango chutney seasoning:
1 cup (250 ml) of mayonnaise
½ cup (155 grams) of organic sweet mango chutney
2 small onions, minced
2 tablespoons of coriander, minced
Freshly ground black pepper

Preparation:
1. Boil the pasta 'al dente' in water with salt. Drain, rinse and drain again.
2. In a salad bowl place the chicken, pasta, chestnuts and mango and mix slightly.
3. Seasoning: In a bowl mix the mayonnaise, chutney, onions, coriander and black pepper. Mix with the salad. Cover and refrigerate until served.

To make this vegan or vegetarian use vegan meat substitute, vegan cheese, and vegan mayonnaise.

Paleo, Wheat free, Low-carb

Sweet Potato Pasta with Avocado Sauce

6 servings

Ingredients:
1 pound (500 grams) sweet potato noodles, spiralized (blade a)
4 oz (125 grams) of peas
4 oz (125 grams) of shredded zucchini (blade c)

Avocado sauce:
1 ripe avocado, seedless and peeled
1 cup (250 grams) of fresh cheese
1 tablespoon of lemon juice
2 teaspoons of finely grated lemon peel
2 tablespoons of coriander, minced
Freshly ground black pepper
Fresh parmesan cheese (optional)

Preparation:
1. Cook the pasta 'al dente' in plenty of boiling water with salt.
Drain and keep hot.
2. Sauce: Blend the avocado with the fresh cheese, lemon juice and
grated peels, coriander and pepper. Set on the side.
3. Steam separately, the peas and the zucchini until soft. Drain well.
Add the vegetables to the hot pasta and mix. Serve the pasta
covering it with the sauce and parmesan peelings (if used).

Use vegan cheese to make vegan

Vegetarian, Paleo, Wheat free, Low-carb, Weight loss

Zucchini Pasta with Fresh Tomato Sauce

4 servings

Ingredients:
1 pound (500 grams) of zucchini noodles, spiralized (blade a)
½ cup of grated parmesan cheese
Handful of baby spinach leaves
Fresh parmesan cheese for garnishing

Fresh tomato sauce:
4 large and ripe tomatoes, diced
½ a cup (60 ml) of vegetable broth
1 tablespoon of white vinegar
Freshly ground black pepper

Preparation:
1. Cook the pasta 'al dente' in plenty of boiling salty water. Drain it and keep it hot.
2. Sauce: Blend the tomatoes with the broth, vinegar and black pepper.
3. Mix the parmesan with the hot pasta. To serve, pour the sauce over the pasta and decorate with watercress leaves and parmesan peelings.

Note
The parmesan cheese peelings give pasta plates an original and elegant touch. Taking a piece of fresh parmesan cheese you get the peelings with a potato peeler or by making thin slices with the cheese grater.

To make vegan use grated vegan cheese

Vegetarian, Paleo, Wheat free, Low-carb, Weight loss

Sweet Potato Noodles with Garlic and Olive Oil

Serves 4

Ingredients:
400g/14oz sweet potato noodles, spiralized (blade a)
6 tbsp extra virgin olive oil
2-4 garlic cloves, crushed
1 dried red chili
1 small handful fresh flat leaf parsley, roughly chopped
Salt

Instructions:
1. Prepare a large pan for cooking the pasta. Cook the pasta in salted boiling water until tender.
2. While waiting for the pasta, in a separate pan, add the olive oil and turn to low heat. Add the crushed garlic and whole dried chili into the heated pan.
3. Stir the garlic and chili until the garlic begins to brown. After that, discard the chili.
4. When the pasta is done, transfer the drained pasta to a large warmed bowl. Pour on the oil and garlic mixture, add the parsley and toss well. Serve immediately.

This is a great base recipe you can add your favorite ingredients too like fresh tomatoes, vegetables, different meats, cheeses etc.

Vegetarian, Paleo, Wheat free, Low-carb, Vegan, Weight loss

Quick Budget Hot Winter Soup

Serves 3

Ingredients:
1 can of condensed tomato soup (salt free)
2 cups potato noodles, spiralized (blade a)
2 cup of zucchini noodles, spiralized (blade a)
1 large onion shredded (blade c)
1 can of sweet corn
3 cups of water (or veggie broth)
Salt to taste
Small amount garlic powder

Directions:
1. Put water (or broth) and condensed tomato soup in a big pot. Add everything else except veggie noodles.
2. Let everything come to a rapid boil. Turn it down to low and let it cook for about 30 minutes.
3. When ready add zucchini and potato noodles, simmer for 5 minutes or until noodles are tender. Serve
4. Taste to see if you have enough salt. If not add more at this time. It is a cheap, healthy, filling soup.

Vegetarian, Paleo, Wheat free, Low-carb, Vegan, Weight loss

Shanghai Cucumber Noodle Salad

4 serves

Ingredients:
2 large cucumbers, topped, spiralize (blade a)
1 large carrot peeled spiralize (blade a)
1 cup rice wine vinegar
1 cup chopped green onions
2 teaspoons minced gingerroot
1 teaspoon Asian sesame oil
1 teaspoon sugar
A teaspoon of red pepper flakes
A teaspoon of salt

Spiralize cucumbers and carrot with your spiralizer.

Instructions:
Combine the cucumbers in a large bowl with the remaining ingredients and toss well. Refrigerate until chilled, about 1 hour (but not longer as the cucumbers could get soggy). Serve

Vegetarian, Paleo, Wheat free, Low-carb, Vegan, Weight loss

Tuscan Pasta Salad with Basil Pesto

Serves 5

Ingredients:
4 medium zucchini, spiralized (blade a)
2 cups basil leaves
⅓ cup of grated Parmesan cheese
¼ cup pine nuts
¼ cup olive oil
2 cloves garlic, pressed
½ teaspoon sea salt
1 cup halved cherry tomatoes
4 ounces feta cheese, crumbled

Preparation

1. Using Blade C on your Spiralizer (or a regular vegetable peeler for wider ribbons), slowly ribbon the zucchini from top to bottom.
2. Place spiralized zucchini in a large bowl and set aside.
3. Prepare the pesto: combine the basil, Parmesan cheese, pine nuts, olive oil, garlic and sea salt in a food processor and pulse until a coarse pesto forms.
4. Carefully toss the zucchini with the pesto. Top with the cherry tomatoes and feta cheese.

Make Vegan with vegan cheese

Vegetarian, Paleo, Wheat free, Low-carb, Weight loss

Vegetarian Zucchini Rice

Serves 2

Ingredients:
2 zucchini spiralized (Blade A) then chopped into rice sized pieces
or blitzed in a processor.
3 cloves garlic, minced
¾ red onion, chopped
1 Tbsp Olive Oil
2½ cup veggie broth
1 Tsp Paprika
1 Tsp Chili Powder

Preparation:
1. Place the saucepan over medium high heat. Add olive oil, red
onion and garlic. Sautee until onion softens, about 5 minutes. Add
zucchini and spices. Sautee until zucchini begins to cook, 5 minutes.
2. Add veggie broth, stir and cover. Reduce to medium low and let
simmer until zucchini rice is tender.
3. Fluff rice with a fork and serve.

Make it meaty with chicken broth

Vegetarian, Paleo, Wheat free, Low-carb, Vegan, Weight loss

Zesty Butternut Squash Minestrone

Serves 6

Ingredients:
2 c butternut squash, peeled, seeded, spiralized (blade a)
1/2 c onions, chopped
2 cloves garlic, minced
20 ounces vegetable broth
1 1/2 cups of water
6 ounces tomato paste
1 tsp Italian seasoning
1/4 tsp black pepper
15 ounces mixed vegetables, canned and drained (or fresh)

Directions:
1. Put onions and garlic in a medium pot and cook until tender.
2. Add broth, water, tomato paste, seasoning, and black pepper to the onions and garlic. Stir and bring to a boil.
3. Reduce heat to low and cook for 10 minutes.
4. Add mixed vegetables and noodles. Bring to a boil.
5. Reduce heat to low and cook ten minutes, or until noodles are done.

6 servings; 50 Calories, 1g Fat, 4g Protein, 12g Carbohydrate, 1g Sodium

You can use chicken broth instead and add cooked, shredded chicken

Vegetarian, Paleo, Wheat free, Low-carb, Vegan, Weight loss

Butternut Squash Pasta Fagioli

8 serves

Ingredients:
8 ounces of butternut squash, peeled, seeded, spiralized (blade b)
2 tablespoons olive oil
1 cup onion, chopped
3 cloves garlic, minced
2 cans Italian-style stewed tomatoes, un-drained
3 cups veggie broth
1 can of cannellini or northern beans, un-drained
¼ cup fresh Italian parsley, chopped
1 teaspoon fresh/dried basil leaves
¼ teaspoon black pepper

Directions:
1. Heat oil in a large pot over medium heat until hot.
2. Add onion and garlic to oil.
3. Sauté for 5 minutes or until onion is tender.
4. Stir in tomatoes with liquid, broth, beans, parsley, basil and pepper.
5. Bring to a boil over high heat, stirring occasionally.
6. Reduce heat to low and simmer, covered for 10 minutes.
7. Add noodles. Continue to simmer, covered for about 10 minutes or until noodles are tender.

For meat eaters you can use chicken broth instead and add cooked, shredded chicken

Per Serving: Calories 120, Total Fat 6 g, Cholesterol 0 mg, Sodium 661 mg, Carbohydrate 17 g, Protein 10 g.

Vegetarian, Paleo, Wheat free, Low-carb, Vegan, Weight loss

Sweet Potato, Zucchini and Onion Soup

Serves 4

Ingredients:
3 cups onions, shredded (blade c)
3 cloves garlic, minced
½ tsp. Stevia or sugar
6 cups veggie broth
1 large zucchini, spiralized (blade b)
1 large sweet potato, spiralized (blade b)
2 Tbsp. dry sherry
¼ tsp. salt
1/8 tsp. black pepper
Parmesan cheese, grated

Directions:
1. Add olive oil to large saucepan heat over medium heat until hot.
2. Add onions and garlic. Cook, covered for about 8 minutes.
3. Add sugar and stir. Cook about 15 minutes.
4. Add broth and bring to a boil.
5. Stir in noodles and simmer, uncovered for about 8 minutes or until tender.
6. Stir in sherry, salt and pepper.

Sprinkle lightly with Parmesan cheese when serving

Serve hot.

You can use chicken broth instead and add cooked, shredded chicken

Vegetarian, Paleo, Wheat free, Low-carb, Weight loss

Creamy Carrot Coleslaw

Serves 6 as sides

This raw coleslaw is perfect for summer cook outs.

Ingredients:
1/2 cup plain Greek yogurt
2 tablespoons Dijon mustard
1 tablespoon water
2 teaspoons mayonnaise
2 teaspoons fresh lemon juice
6 cups thinly shredded cabbage (blade c)
4 medium carrots, shredded (blade c)
1 cup thinly shredded red onion (blade c)
1/2 teaspoon chia seeds

Directions:
1. Whisk together yogurt, mustard, water, mayonnaise, and lemon juice in a large bowl.
2. Add remaining ingredients and toss to combine well. Season the coleslaw with salt and pepper.

Coleslaw may be made 1 day ahead and chilled if covered.

Each serving about 60 calories and 1.1 gram fat (15% of calories from fat)

You can make a vegan with vegan mayo, or swap mayo for balsamic

Vegetarian, Paleo, Wheat free, Low-carb, Weight loss

Healthy Raw Beet and Sweet Potato Salad

Serves 5

Ingredients:
2 large sweet potatoes (spiralized blade a)
3 medium beets (spiralized blade a)
3 scallions sliced
½ of a cup slivered almonds
Balsamic Vinegar

Directions:
1. Peel the sweet potatoes and the beets. Cut off ends. Then spiralize into long noodles. Cut the spirals to desired length.
2. Mix the sweet potato and beets together in a bowl. Then cut the scallion into small slices. Sprinkle the salad with the scallions. Serve with balsamic vinegar or your favorite vinaigrette.

In case you're wondering, yes you can eat spiralized beets and sweet potato raw. In fact when you cook them you lose a lot of the nutritional value of these veggies.

Raw, Vegetarian, Paleo, Wheat free, Low-carb, Weight loss

Casablanca Sweet Potato Stew

Serves 5

Ingredients:
1 tablespoon olive oil
1 large onion, shredded (blade c)
2 cups shredded cabbage (blade c)
4 sweet potatoes spiralized (blade a)
3 to 4 cloves garlic, minced
14 ½ ounces diced fresh tomatoes
1 1/2 cups tomato juice
3/4 cup apple juice
1 to 2 teaspoons grated fresh ginger root
1/4 to 1/2 teaspoon red pepper flakes
2 cups fresh/frozen cut green beans
1/3 cup natural peanut butter

Directions:
1. Heal oil in a large skillet over medium-high heat.
2. Add onion; Cook, stirring, until tender, about 5 minutes.
3. Add cabbage and garlic; Cook, stirring, until cabbage is tender, 5 minutes.
4. Stir in tomatoes, tomato juice, apple juice, ginger, and red pepper flakes.
5. Reduce heat to medium-low; Cover.
6. Simmer until hot and bubbling, about 5 minutes.
7. Stir in noodles and green beans and simmer, uncovered, for 3 minutes.
8. Stir in peanut butter until well blended and hot, about 1 minute.

Serve stew with a salad, or spoon it on couscous.

About 100 calories per serve

Vegetarian, Paleo, Wheat free, Low-carb, Weight loss

Kagawa Zucchini Udon Noodle Soup

Serves 2

There's nothing better than a steaming bowl of hot zucchini noodle soup on a cold winter evening and this recipe will have you out of the kitchen in 10 minutes.

Feel free to add your favorite extras like cooked shredded chicken or pork, other vegetables or an egg.

Because zucchini noodles are a little oilier than egg noodles you do not need to add vegetable oil to stop them sticking.

Ingredients:
2 bowls of veggie broth
2 zucchinis, spiralized, Udon size (blade b)
1 tablespoon soya sauce
2 small pieces of dried seaweed
2 tablespoons of chopped spring onions

Directions:
1. Cook the zucchini udon noodles in a pot of water. Cook till al dente, drain and then plunge into a bowl of cold water for a few seconds. Drain again and place in a serving bowl.
2. Heat the soup broth up and pour over the zucchini noodles in the bowl.
3. Add the soya sauce, chopped spring onions and dried seaweed.

You can use chicken broth instead

Vegetarian, Paleo, Wheat free, Low-carb, Weight loss

Raw Vegan Zesty Cucumber Ribbon Salad

If you are looking for a healthy vegan recipe this raw cucumber ribbon salad may be your perfect quick lunch.

Ingredients
½ can coconut milk (approx 200 ml)
2 cloves garlic, pressed
1 lemon, zested and juiced
1 Tbsp dill (fresh or dried)
Pinch black pepper
Small amount of grated red onion
1 cucumber, peeled, seeded, ribboned (blade c)
3 stalks celery, chopped

How to prepare the cucumber salad

In salad bowl prepare your dressing by mixing the ingredients together. Add the vegetables and toss.

Serve this cucumber salad immediately as a light lunch for 2, or 1 if you are a piggy.

Vegetarian, Paleo, Wheat free, Low-carb, Weight loss

Asian Fusion Cucumber Noodle Salad

Serves 2

This is a simple, quick, light Asian fusion cucumber salad.

Ingredients:
1 cucumber, seeded, spiralized (blade b)
1/4 cup rice vinegar
1/2 tsp of sesame oil
A dash of ginger juice / fresh ginger
1 tsp of sugar
A pinch of black pepper

Directions:
1. Spiralize the cucumber into noodles (blade b) and put it in a large bowl.
2. In a small bowl place the rice vinegar, sesame oil, shot of ginger juice / fresh ginger, sugar, and black pepper and mix together.
3. Pour the dressing over the cucumber and toss it.

Serve as a side or main and very nice with Asian dishes.

Vegetarian, Paleo, Wheat free, Low-carb, Weight loss

Raw Carrot Noodles with Zesty Lime Peanut Sauce

Total Prep Time: 15 minutes
Serves 4 people

Ingredients:
For the raw carrot noodles:
4 large carrots, peeled, topped and spiralized into noodles (blade a)
1/4 cup of slivered almonds
1/2 cup fresh cilantro, finely chopped

For the Lime Peanut Sauce:
2 tablespoons organic peanut butter
4 tablespoons coconut milk
Pinch cayenne
2 cloves garlic, peeled, finely chopped
1 tbsp fresh ginger, peeled and grated
2 tbsp lime juice
Sea salt to taste

Instructions:
To Make the Lime Peanut Sauce:
1. Combine all ingredients in a small bowl and mix together until smooth and creamy.

To Prepare the Carrot Pasta:
2. Wash carrots, peel them, and pat them dry.
3. Spiralize noodles out of all of the carrots. (blade a).
4. Place all carrot noodles into a large serving bowl. Pour the Lime Peanut Sauce over the noodles and gently toss together (Use your hands for this part).
5. Serve with slivered almonds (or peanuts) and freshly chopped cilantro.

Vegetarian, Paleo, Wheat free, Low-carb, Weight loss

Oriental Chicken with Carrot Noodles

Serves 3

Ingredients:
2 skinless chicken breasts cut into slivers
1 onion, peeled, shredded (blade c)
2 small carrots, peeled, spiralized (blade b)
1 large zucchini, spiralized (blade b)
1 cup mushrooms, sliced
2 tbsp. peanut oil
2 garlic clove
4 tbsp of low sodium soy sauce

Preparation:
1. Heat oil in a large skillet or wok.
2. Stir fry onion, mushrooms, garlic and sliced chicken for 10 minutes and lower heat to medium and cook until chicken is cooked through.
3. Turn up heat and stir fry veggie noodles with other ingredients for 5 more minutes, or until noodles are tender
4. Take off heat then toss with soy sauce and serve.

Paleo, Wheat free, Low-carb, Weight loss

Zucchini Spaghetti and Meatballs

Serves 6 as main (can freeze leftovers)

6 zucchinis, spiralized (blade a) set aside

For Meatballs:
1/2 pound each, Ground Beef, Pork and Lamb
1/2 cup Breadcrumbs (Homemade or Store Bought)
3-4 cloves Garlic, minced
1 egg
1/2 cup Freshly Grated Parmigiano Cheese (or generic)
1/4 cup Whole Milk
Salt and Freshly Ground Pepper to Taste

For the Red Sauce:
16 ounces Tomato Puree
8 ounces Tomato paste
1 White Onion, diced
3 cloves Garlic, minced
1/4 cup Sugar
1 Bay Leaf
1/2 tablespoon Crushed Red Pepper Flakes
Salt and Freshly Ground Pepper to Taste

Method:
Mix ingredients for meatballs, be careful not to over mix. Roll meat mixture into golf ball size balls and set aside. In large, heavy bottom pan, heat 1/2 cup olive oil on medium heat.

Brown the meatballs in batches, being careful not to crowd the pan. 8-10 minutes per batch. Remove meatballs and allow to rest.

Drain off left over pan drippings reserving 2 tablespoons. Return pan to medium heat and add onion and garlic. Sauté until onions are translucent, do not overcook, or garlic will become bitter. Add remaining ingredients and simmer over low heat for one hour.

Cook zucchini noodles in boiling water until tender and add to the sauce with 1/4 cup of the noodle cooking water. Allow to cook 1-2 minutes. Add meatballs and stir to coat. Transfer the entire mixture to a heated platter and garnish with more cheese and chopped fresh parsley.

Once you have mastered the Red Sauce above the ways you can use it are endless. You can use it in lasagnas and over all types of veggie noodles.

Paleo, Wheat free, Low-carb

Conclusion

Thank you for buying my eBook and investing in a healthier way of cooking for you and your family.

I hope you enjoy the recipes and try most of them out, I am sure your family will love the healthy, tasty meals you make with your spiralizer.

Don't forget that this is just the first of a series of cookbooks I am writing for you on spiralizer recipes and topics.

Perhaps you may want to become a member of the spiralizer community by joining my newsletter, you will be informed of upcoming books and also get new spiralizer recipes and tips. LINK

Please Leave a Review

Finally I would appreciate it greatly if you left a review of my spiralizer eBook on Kindle Amazon, the more reviews I get the more people like you will find my message and make a positive step towards healthier cooking.

Happy Spiralizing

Katey Goodrich

Made in the USA
Lexington, KY
24 February 2015